SCIENCE
ESSENTIALS
CHEMISTRY

# Geological
# Change

Denise Walker

Evans

EVANS
LONDON

© Evans Brothers Ltd 2007

Published by:
**Evans Brothers**
**2a Portman Mansions**
**Chiltern Street**
**London W1U 6NR**

Series editor:
**Harriet Brown**

Editor:
**Harriet Brown**

Design:
**Robert Walster**

Illustrations:
**Peter Bull Art Studio**

Printed in China by
WKT Company Limited

British Library Cataloguing in
Publication Data

Walker, Denise
  Geological change. - (Science
essentials. Chemistry)
  1. Geochemistry - Juvenile literature
  I. Title
  551.9

ISBN-10: 0-237-53000-7

ISBN-13: 978-0-237-53000-6

# Contents

# Introduction

Planet Earth is constantly changing. The continents are drifting on a sea of fluid rock, water is eroding the land and our climate is warming. We depend on the Earth's resources for food, water, shelter, and for building structures and devices that we take for granted every day.

This book takes you on a journey to discover more about the wonderful world of geology. Find out how the Universe formed and discover how elements were created. Take a closer look at the Earth's rocky crust, how it has formed over millions of years and how it provides us with the materials we use in our everyday lives. Find out how the Earth looked millions of years ago and discover how ice ages and plate tectonics have resulted in the Earth we know today. You can also find out how geology has contributed to famous natural and man-made structures, such as the Grand Canyon and the Taj Mahal.

This book also contains feature boxes that will help you to unravel more about the mysteries of geology. Test yourself on what you have learnt so far; investigate some of the concepts discussed; find out more key facts; and discover some of the scientific findings of the past and how these might be utilised in the future.

Geology is all around us. Now you can understand how our planet has become the wonder that it is today.

## DID YOU KNOW?

▶ Watch out for these boxes – they contain surprising and fascinating facts about the geology of planet Earth.

## TEST YOURSELF

▶ Use these boxes to see how much you've learnt. Try to answer the questions without looking at the book, but take a look if you are really stuck.

## INVESTIGATE

▶ These boxes contain experiments that you can carry out at home. The equipment you will need is usually cheap and easy to find.

## TIME TRAVEL

▶ These boxes describe scientific discoveries from the past, and fascinating developments that pave the way for the advance of science in the future.

### ANSWERS

At the end of this book on pages 46 and 47, you will find the answers to questions from the 'Test yourself' and 'Investigate' boxes.

### GLOSSARY

Words highlighted in **bold** are described in detail in the glossary on pages 46 and 47.

# Formation of the Earth

Many scientists believe that the Universe was created around 13.7 billion years ago by a fantastic explosion called the Big Bang. This theory states that all matter, space, time and energy were once concentrated into an unimaginably dense ball, called a primeval atom. The scientists believe that the primeval atom exploded to create our Universe.

### WHAT IS AN ATOM?

An atom is a tiny particle. Everything around us is made from atoms. An atom contains a central nucleus. The nucleus is made from protons and neutrons. Electrons surround the nucleus.

### WHAT IS AN ELEMENT?

An element is a group of atoms that have a unique number of protons in each nucleus. Each element has a specific name. For example, oxygen is an element. Oxygen atoms have eight protons in their nucleus. The lightest elements are:

(1) Hydrogen, which has one proton in its nucleus.

(2) Helium, which has two protons in its nucleus.

(3) Lithium, which has three protons in its nucleus. All other elements have grown from these three elements. Today, we know of 116 elements.

### BEYOND THE BIG BANG

(1) Scientists now believe that for the first 400,000 years of its existence, the Universe was too hot for any elements to form. At temperatures that ranged from several million **Kelvin** to 100 billion Kelvin, atoms burst apart. Instead, the early Universe was made of **plasma**. Plasma is similar to a gas but it is so hot that the electrons are ripped away from the nuclei. A plasma consists of loose electrons and nuclei (protons and neutrons).

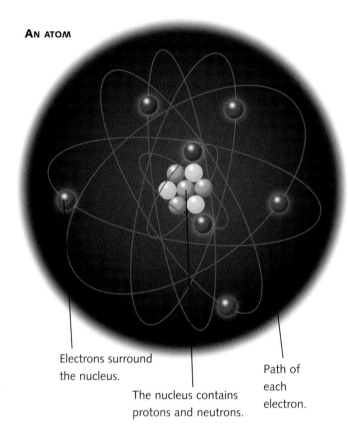

AN ATOM

Electrons surround the nucleus.

The nucleus contains protons and neutrons.

Path of each electron.

(2) After the first 400,000 years, the Universe became cool enough for simple atoms to form. Electrons, protons and neutrons from the original explosion fused together to form atoms. This stage is called 'recombination'.

(3) The simple atoms began to combine and clump together. Stars eventually formed from clouds of gas under the force of gravity. Any matter that did not form a star revolved around it as a thin disc of dust.

(4) Planets are believed to have formed gradually

from these thin discs. The matter clumped together and became denser until it collapsed inwards to form an early type of planet called a protoplanet. Eventually, the star blew away most of the rest of the thin disc to leave the planet behind. Planets grew larger as they collided and fused with other bodies. (5) Planet Earth formed around 4.6 billion years ago. It was initially molten, but as it cooled, the outer layer hardened to form a crust. Beneath the crust is the molten mantle. Beneath the mantle is the outer core which is still molten, but more viscous than the mantle. Finally, at the centre of planet Earth is the solid inner core.

## HOW DID THE FORMATION OF THE UNIVERSE CREATE ELEMENTS?

Elements are formed by **nuclear fusion** reactions. During normal chemical reactions, it is the outer parts of the atom, the electrons, which move to (or are shared with) other atoms. This forms chemical bonds between atoms to create new substances. However, at very hot temperatures,

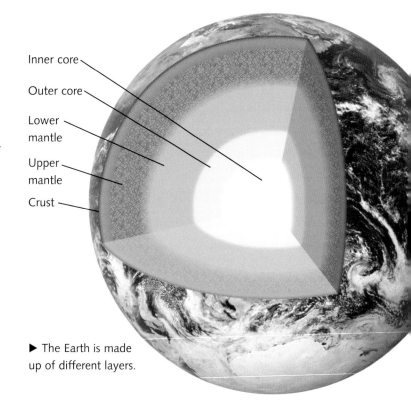

Inner core
Outer core
Lower mantle
Upper mantle
Crust

▶ The Earth is made up of different layers.

such as those that exist inside stars, electrons are stripped from the atoms. The nuclei themselves are forced together to produce larger nuclei of different elements.

Even heavier elements are generated from bigger, hotter stars called 'blue giants'. However, in a star's life there is a point when the star cannot make any more heavy elements. At this point, the star can no longer support the weight of its outer parts. The star collapses in a massive implosion and a shock wave then blows most of the star apart. But at that split second, it produces all of the heavier elements, up to and including the heaviest element of all, uranium. This is called a **supernova** and it distributes all the star's material throughout the galaxy. Luckily for us, the Sun won't implode because it is too small. The supernovae of giant stars created many of the heavier elements found on planet Earth.

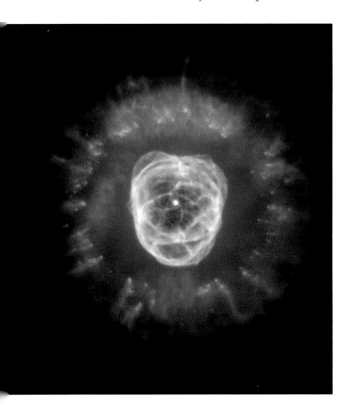

◀ This dying star has formed the Eskimo Nebula. It is flinging material far into space. It began forming around 10,000 years ago.

# The Earth's rocky crust

The Earth's crust is composed of many different types of rock. Rocks are naturally-occurring aggregates (clumps) of minerals. Minerals are natural chemical compounds formed through geological processes. Geological processes result in three main types of rock – **sedimentary**, **igneous** and **metamorphic**.

## SEDIMENTARY ROCKS

Sedimentary rocks cover about five per cent of the Earth's crust and take thousands of millions of years to form:

(1) Rocks and the remains of living creatures are broken down into smaller particles by natural forces such as rain, wind and river currents.

(2) As the rocks become smaller, the tiny sediments can be carried to a place where the natural force no longer operates.

(3) The pieces of rock stop moving and settle down. Rock particles that were in solution return to their solid form when any water evaporates. The pieces of rock are now called sediments.

(4) Over time, layers of sediment build up. Older sediment forms the bottom layers and newer sediment piles on top.

(5) Eventually, the weight of the layers compresses the sediment beneath. Under such pressure, the water is squeezed out and this cements the sediments together. Sedimentary rock has formed.

The sediment can be derived from clay, silt, sand, gravel or pebbles. Clay produces a sedimentary rock called mudstone. The individual particles are tiny. Mudstone that splits easily into very thin layers is called shale. Mudrock, mudstone and shale form 65 per cent of the Earth's sedimentary rock.

▼ Layers of sedimentary rock can be clearly seen in the Horseshoe Canyon, Alberta, Canada.

## CHARACTERISTICS OF SEDIMENTARY ROCKS

Sedimentary rocks have the following features:

▶ The rock appears in layers in its natural surroundings. These layers represent the different sediments that have been added over time.

▶ Sedimentary rocks may contain fossils. Fossils are the preserved remains of ancient plants and animals. Sedimentary rocks contain fossils because, unlike other rocks, they form at temperatures and pressures that do not destroy animal and plant remains.

▶ On closer inspection, sedimentary rocks have a grainy appearance. If you rub sedimentary rocks between your fingers they may also feel grainy. These grains are the actual sediments that form the rocks.

▶ These fossils are in sedimentary rock that is between 8 and 12 million years old.

## DID YOU KNOW?

▶ In 2004, scientists studying rocks from Antarctica found a fossil that came from a previously unidentified species of plant-eating dinosaur. The dinosaur was a primitive sauropod, similar to a diplodocus. The fossil dinosaur appears to be at least 170 million years old. The fossil was a hip bone and from this, scientists concluded that the creature was around two metres tall and over nine metres long.

## EXAMPLES OF SEDIMENTARY ROCKS

We call rocks made from the remains of living creatures, 'biogenic sedimentary rocks'. Limestone is mainly made of calcium carbonate from the shells of marine organisms. When the organisms died, they fell to the seabed and created calcium carbonate sediment. Eventually, the sediment became incorporated into limestone rock.

Coal is an extremely important sedimentary rock. It is made from the remains of ancient ferns and trees. When these plants died, their materials were compressed and heated in the Earth's crust over millions of years. Eventually, they turned into coal.

Precipitates are another type of sedimentary rock. They form when solutions evaporate and leave the sedimentary rock behind. Gypsum is a precipitate. It is used to make plasterboard for house building because it is fire-resistant. In its natural state it contains water. When it is heated, the water is released as steam. Its temperature does not rise and it does not burn until the water has been released.

## TEST YOURSELF

▶ Describe in your own words how sedimentary rocks are formed.
▶ Try to find out the names of three more sedimentary rocks. Are the rocks you have found biogenic, precipitate or neither?

## A CLOSER LOOK AT LIMESTONE

Limestone rock, which is a sedimentary rock, forms spectacular rocky outcrops and islands all over the world. For example, the white cliffs of Dover in the UK, the Niagara Escarpment on the Canadian/USA border and the Ha Long Bay National Park in Vietnam are all formed from limestone. Limestone has a number of important uses in the building industry and in agriculture, and it is the source of many everyday chemicals. But before we can use it, **geologists** must extract it from the ground.

## LIMESTONE MINING

Limestone is extracted from the ground in a process called quarrying. Often, limestone is found at sites of particular natural beauty. Unfortunately, quarrying has an irreversible effect on the environment. Limestone is blasted from the ground with explosives. Quarrying in this way creates noise and dust pollution and may interfere with the natural habitats of plant and animal species. However, quarrying can bring employment and much needed revenue to some otherwise disadvantaged areas.

▼ These magnificent rocky outcrops in Ha Long Bay, Vietnam, are made from limestone.

Once the limestone has been quarried, vegetation is replanted in an attempt to re-populate the area with plant and animal species. The quarry may fill with groundwater to create a lake. The idea is that over time, the natural environment of the area may be restored.

## TREATING THE LIMESTONE

The extracted limestone is heated in a lime kiln. The temperature inside the lime kiln is about 1,500°C. At high temperatures, limestone breaks down into calcium oxide and carbon dioxide. The calcium oxide (sometimes called quicklime) is released through the bottom of the kiln and the carbon dioxide escapes from the top in the form of a gas.

## REACTIONS OF LIMESTONE

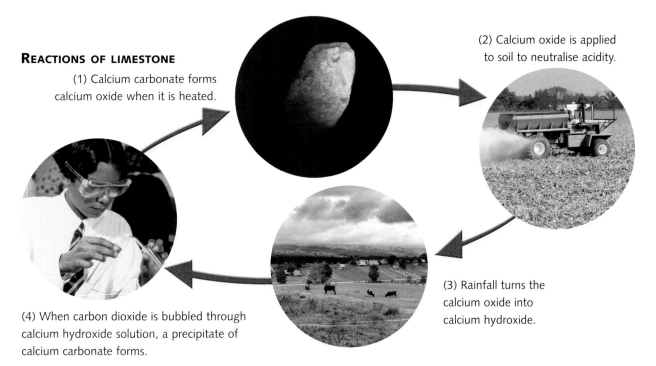

(1) Calcium carbonate forms calcium oxide when it is heated.

(2) Calcium oxide is applied to soil to neutralise acidity.

(3) Rainfall turns the calcium oxide into calcium hydroxide.

(4) When carbon dioxide is bubbled through calcium hydroxide solution, a precipitate of calcium carbonate forms.

(1) Limestone glows brightly when it is heated to produce calcium oxide, or quicklime. This light was used in theatres before the age of electric lights – hence the expression 'in the limelight'.

(2) Lime is used in agriculture to neutralise soil acidity. When farmers grow field crops, plants remove nutrients from the soil. This makes the soil acidic. Farmers must replace the lost nutrients and re-establish neutral soil. Lime is an alkaline substance and when placed into acidic soil, the soil becomes neutral again.

(3) When water is added to lime, a new compound is formed. This is called calcium hydroxide, or slaked lime. When rain falls on a lime-treated field, the slaked lime works its way deeper into the soil.

(4) When a lot of water is added to slaked lime, calcium hydroxide solution (or limewater) is formed. You may have seen bottles of limewater in your school laboratory because it is used to test for the presence of carbon dioxide. When carbon dioxide gas is bubbled through limewater, it turns milky. A fine precipitate of calcium carbonate forms, bringing us back to where we started.

## OTHER USES OF LIMESTONE:

▶ **Building blocks**. Limestone is widely available, long-lasting and can be easily cut into blocks, which make it suitable for constructing buildings.

▶ **Cement**. Limestone is heated with clay and calcium sulphate (gypsum) to make cement.

▶ **Concrete**. Concrete is made by mixing cement, sand and small stones together with water. It is a common building material that is used to make foundations for buildings, block bricks, roads, pavements and as a base for fence posts. It was first invented by the Romans over 2,000 years ago. They discovered that by mixing sandy volcanic ash and lime mortar combined with sand and gravel, they obtained a hard and waterproof synthetic rock surface. Without concrete, it would not have been possible to build the Colosseum in Rome, Italy – one of the first buildings to use concrete – in the 70s AD.

▲ The Colosseum is made of limestone, brick and concrete.

## IGNEOUS ROCKS

Igneous rocks are formed when melted rock cools or solidifies. This happens either within the Earth's crust or on the Earth's surface. The rock's formation requires specific temperatures and pressures. The word 'igneous' comes from the Latin word for fire — 'ignis'. There are over 700 types of igneous rock and they make up approximately 95 per cent of the upper part of the Earth's crust.

### ORIGIN OF IGNEOUS ROCKS

The uppermost layer of the Earth, the crust, extends 35 kilometres down under the continents. Beneath the oceans, the crust is about 10 kilometres thick. Beneath this layer of solid rock there is a layer of **magma** (molten rock) called the mantle. The mantle is almost 3,000 kilometres thick and is constantly moving. Hotter material from nearer the centre of the Earth moves upwards towards the crust, cools and then sinks back downwards. This cycle is called a **convection current**. Convection currents cause the movement of the Earth's crust in much the same way as oil moves on heated water.

As magma moves upwards towards the Earth's surface one of two things can happen.
(1) The magma can find its way between cracks in the Earth's surface and be expelled into the atmosphere. When the **lava** cools it forms rock that we call extrusive igneous rock. This lava is often expelled from a volcano, but can also ooze from cracks (see page 33) beneath the sea.
(2) The magma moves towards the Earth's surface but does not appear above the ground. However, as temperatures are cooler just beneath the surface than further down, the magma can cool to form rock that we call intrusive igneous rock.

▼ This cross-section of the Earth's crust shows where igneous rocks form.

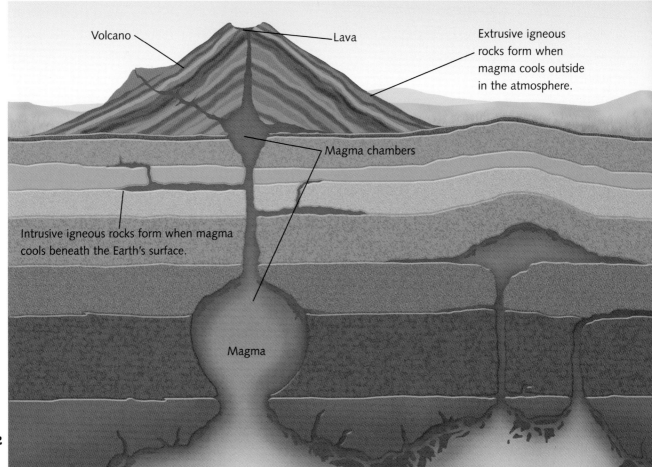

Volcano

Lava

Extrusive igneous rocks form when magma cools outside in the atmosphere.

Magma chambers

Intrusive igneous rocks form when magma cools beneath the Earth's surface.

Magma

## IMPORTANCE OF IGNEOUS ROCKS

▶ The minerals found within igneous rocks and their location provide clues about the composition, and temperature and pressure conditions of the mantle.

▶ The age of the rocks can be determined using dating techniques. Scientists measure the quantities of radioactive elements within the rocks. Radioactive elements break down at a known rate. If scientists measure the quantity of the radioactive elements still present, it is possible to discover the age of the rock.

▶ Some igneous rocks are sources of important materials such as tin, tungsten and uranium.

## CHARACTERISTICS OF IGNEOUS ROCKS

Granite is an igneous rock. On closer inspection, you can see that granite is composed of crystals. The crystals form when the molten magma cools. The longer the time period over which cooling occurs, the larger the crystals grow. Intrusive igneous rocks form at warm temperatures and this is why crystallisation takes a little longer. Granite usually occurs in massive chunks and is hard and tough. This makes it ideal for widespread use as a construction stone.

Basalt is an extrusive igneous rock. When magma is exposed to the cool temperatures of our atmosphere, it cools very quickly giving the basalt rock a very small crystal size. The shape, structure and texture of basalt depends on the way it erupted and where it erupted. For example, lava can erupt into the sea or the air, it can erupt in an explosive manner or it can creep down the volcano as a lava flow. Some extrusive igneous rocks are expelled from volcanoes so quickly that they do not have time to form even small crystals. Volcanic glass called obsidian forms in this way.

▲ Granite usually forms at depths of between 1.5 and 50 kilometres within the Earth's crust

▼ Columns of basalt form when thick lava flows cool. This results in fractures, usually in a hexagonal pattern.

# METAMORPHIC ROCKS

Metamorphic rocks are created when sedimentary and igneous rocks change their form. The word 'metamorphic' comes from the Greek words 'meta', meaning change, and 'morphe', meaning form. Metamorphic rocks form beneath the Earth's surface. The majority of metamorphic rocks are formed from sedimentary rocks because these rocks are naturally pushed further into the Earth's mantle where it is hot and pressurised. Igneous rocks are naturally pushed towards the outer, cooler parts of the Earth, but in some instances they can turn into metamorphic rocks.

## ORIGIN OF METAMORPHIC ROCKS

The Earth's crust moves as a result of convection currents in the molten mantle below. During this movement, surface rock can be buried and pushed into the mantle. When this happens, the rock experiences high temperatures and great pressures. Under these extreme conditions, its structure changes and it forms metamorphic rock. Marble forms in this way from the sedimentary rock limestone, and slate forms from the sedimentary rock mudstone.

## FORMATION OF MARBLE

A process called **recrystallisation** is responsible for the formation of marble. Recrystallisation changes the size of the particles found in the rock. Limestone and marble are both composed of the same chemical compound – calcium carbonate – but the crystal structure is different.

During recrystallisation, high temperatures allow the rock's atoms to move more freely. They are not as free to move as if they were in a liquid, but free enough to re-organise themselves into a new pattern. The high pressure helps to squash the atoms into their new arrangements. The small calcite crystals change into an interlocking mosaic of larger marble crystals.

▼ Limestone, a sedimentary rock, has a coarse texture.

▼ Marble, a metamorphic rock, has a smooth texture.

## FORMATION OF QUARTZITE

In sandstone, the quartz sand grains recrystallise into large interlocking crystals to form very compact quartzite. The high temperatures and pressures involved in the process of metamorphism destroys any fossil material present in the sedimentary rock.

▲ This quartzite crag is perfect for rock climbing.

## BUILDING WITH METAMORPHIC ROCK

The Taj Mahal, built in India between 1632 and 1654, is a man-made structure composed almost entirely from marble, a metamorphic rock. It took over 20,000 workmen 11 years to complete the mausoleum itself, and a further 11 years to complete the surrounding wall, mosque, gateway and minarets (towers). Marble is an ideal building material because it is incredibly hard. The lack of spaces in its crystal structure means that it cannot easily be chipped or cracked and it will resist attack from wind, rain and extremes of temperature.

The designer of the Taj Mahal clearly appreciated the very hard and heavy composition of marble, because the surrounding turrets are angled slightly away from the mausoleum itself. If they were to fall, they would fall away from the main body of the building, limiting any damage.

## SLATE

Slate is another metamorphic rock. When it forms from mudstone, the particles are recrystallised into fine layers that can be shorn from one another. Slate can be extracted from a slate quarry by splitting the material into thin sheets. It makes a good roof tile as it can easily be made into thin sheets that are hard and waterproof. Unfortunately, roof tiles are not hard enough to resist breakage when they fall to the ground during a storm. You can examine the sheet-like structure of slate when this occurs because the roof tiles always break into even finer sheets.

▼ A 15-kilometre earth ramp was built to transport the marble and other materials from the city of Agra, India, to the Taj Mahal construction site.

# 3

# Changing rocks

Rocks not only change their form as a result of the movement of the Earth's crust. **Weathering** and **erosion** also change rocks. Weathering is the process by which rocks are broken down when exposed to physical, chemical or biological processes. Erosion is the movement of rocks, and the products of weathering, by water, ice, wind or gravity.

## PHYSICAL WEATHERING

A common type of physical weathering is called freeze-thaw. It occurs in places that have freezing cold nights and warmer days. Water works its way into small cracks in the rock. At night, the water freezes and expands. This forces the cracks wider and deeper into the rock. During the day, the ice thaws, and more water can fill the expanded cracks. The cycle repeats itself over and over again until eventually the cracks become so large that the rocks can fracture.

◄ This granite in the Cairngorms in Scotland has been weathered by freeze-thaw.

Another type of physical weathering is called onion skin weathering, or thermal expansion. In hot desert climates, temperatures vary massively between day and night. This range can be up to 25°C over a 24-hour period. The rock heats up and expands during the day. During the cold night, the rocks contract and this causes stress on the outer layers. Thin skin-like pieces of rock peel off under this stress.

◄ This pebble has undergone onion skin weathering. The outer layer has been removed in places.

## CHEMICAL WEATHERING

Acid, water and oxygen chemically attack rocks. Rain is a very weak acidic solution because it contains carbon dioxide from our atmosphere. Sedimentary rocks that contain carbonates are particularly susceptible to acid attack. The carbonates react with the rain and produce soluble and gaseous products. The rock is eventually worn away. As rain water passes through soil, it dissolves the many minerals present there, which makes the water even more acidic. The effects of chemical weathering form caves and caverns.

Water, acidic or not, can also attack other rocks. For example, when it rains on granite, water reacts with some of granite's minerals and causes it to break down into smaller particles of clay, which are then washed away. This is only a problem if the granite is exposed to rain for long periods of time.

Iron-containing rocks rust when oxygen and water are present. Brown streaks in a rock face indicate that rusting has taken place. Rusting can weaken the structure and cause small pieces of rock to break away.

## BIOLOGICAL WEATHERING

Plants and trees can take root in small cracks in a rock's surface, even if the crack only contains a tiny amount of soil. The roots can grow deep into

▲ Caves and archways are common in limestone cliffs.

the rock, which weakens it and causes it to break up. Lichen and mosses grow on bare rock surfaces, which turns the rock face into a more humid micro-environment. This increases the physical and chemical breakdown of the rock.

Animals can also cause rock damage. Burrowing animals remove soil layers that cover rocks. This exposes the rock to physical and chemical weathering. In addition, when animals die and decompose, their remains create a more acidic soil, which aids the chemical weathering of rock.

## EROSION

The tiny particles of rock that form as a result of weathering are called sediments. Erosion is when the sediments are worn away by the following processes:

▶ Gravity – Sediments fall from cliffs and mountain sides.

▶ Wind – Wind carries loose, small and light sediments such as desert sand.

▶ Water – Crashing waves from the sea or ocean are responsible for the erosion of cliffs and the creation of caves. A fast-flowing river is powerful enough to carry large pebble-sized sediments, as well as much smaller sediments. Rivers slow down as they near the sea or ocean. Sediments are often deposited at the river mouth, which can cause the river to silt up to form a delta. When a river drops off its load, this is called deposition.

▶ Ice – Glaciers can scrape slowly down a slope and break up the rock over which they travel. Some glaciers can travel one metre in one day.

▼ The Hubbard Glacier enters the ocean off Alaska, USA.

# THE ROCK CYCLE

Metamorphic, igneous and sedimentary rocks form and change over millions of years. This series of changes is called the rock cycle.

## INVESTIGATE

▶ Find out what 'porous' and 'non-porous' mean in terms of rocks. Which rock type is best for building?

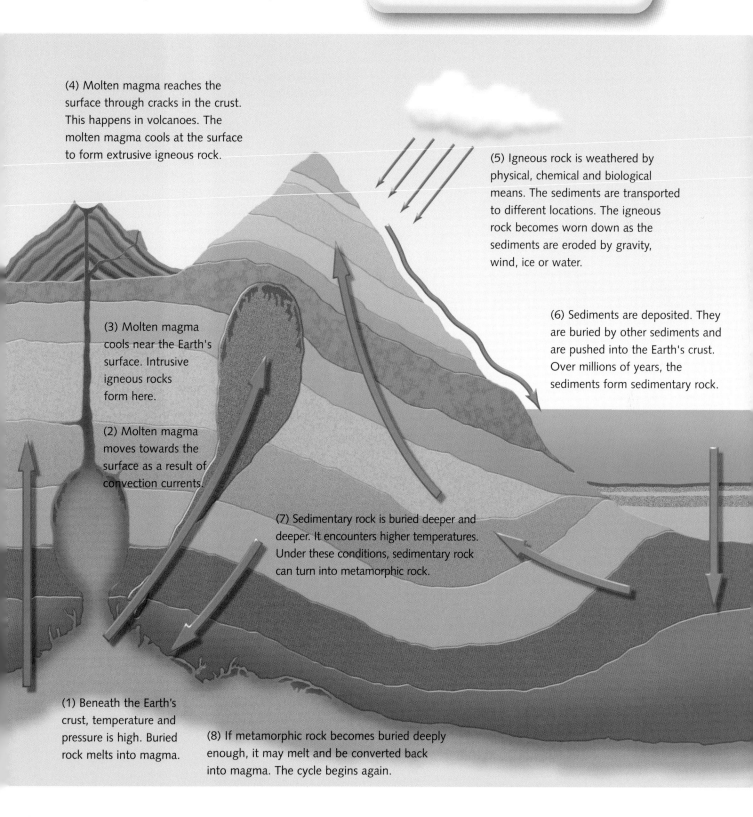

(4) Molten magma reaches the surface through cracks in the crust. This happens in volcanoes. The molten magma cools at the surface to form extrusive igneous rock.

(5) Igneous rock is weathered by physical, chemical and biological means. The sediments are transported to different locations. The igneous rock becomes worn down as the sediments are eroded by gravity, wind, ice or water.

(3) Molten magma cools near the Earth's surface. Intrusive igneous rocks form here.

(6) Sediments are deposited. They are buried by other sediments and are pushed into the Earth's crust. Over millions of years, the sediments form sedimentary rock.

(2) Molten magma moves towards the surface as a result of convection currents.

(7) Sedimentary rock is buried deeper and deeper. It encounters higher temperatures. Under these conditions, sedimentary rock can turn into metamorphic rock.

(1) Beneath the Earth's crust, temperature and pressure is high. Buried rock melts into magma.

(8) If metamorphic rock becomes buried deeply enough, it may melt and be converted back into magma. The cycle begins again.

# TIME TRAVEL: THE GRAND CANYON

The Grand Canyon in Arizona, USA, is around 445 kilometres long, 30 kilometres wide and nearly 2 kilometres deep. It is formed of a series of layers of sedimentary rock. The oldest layers date back 1.7 billion years, and these rocks are exposed at the very bottom of the canyon. But how did the interesting rock strata, canyon shape and vivid colours of the Grand Canyon actually form?

Only five of the ten men completed the journey. The other five gave up because they felt they had already had enough adventure to last them a lifetime. Powell succeeded in confirming his theory that the river existed before the canyon, and that it had cut its way through the rock. In 1871, he repeated the journey, and this time he made the first accurate map of the area.

▲ Sunset at the Grand Canyon highlights the sedimentary rock layers.

### THE FIRST EXPLORATION

In 1869, the geologist John Wesley Powell took a legendary journey down the Colorado River. He was the first person to study the canyon. He took nine men, four boats and supplies for ten months down the river. When it rained, the river ran thick with red sediment carried by the tributaries that joined the main channel of the river. It was a perilous journey that took three months to complete.

### FORMATION OF THE SEDIMENTARY ROCK

The exact details regarding the formation of the Grand Canyon are still highly controversial and debated by geologists. The layers of sedimentary rock are believed to have mostly formed below sea level between two billion and 230 million years ago. Warm shallow seas and swamps deposited layers of mud, sand and lime as the shoreline repeatedly advanced and retreated. The layers became compressed and folded. Limestone from the shells of sea animals as well as fossils of trilobites, marine worms and jellyfish can be found in the canyon's rock. At one time, there was even a desert in the area, which deposited a layer of sand. This has since been compressed into sandstone.

The uppermost layers of the canyon contain much red rock produced from shale, siltstone and sandstone. Some of the layers contain impressions of fern leaves, raindrops and insect wings. The red colour is also produced by the presence of iron oxide compounds which have leached out of other rocks, and run down the side of the canyon, staining the rock beneath. The very top layers contain a lot of sandstone. Some of the sand particles were transported to the canyon by the wind and deposited in what became the sandstone layers.

▲ The Colorado River cuts through the Grand Canyon.

### UPLIFT AND EROSION

Around 65 million years ago, the Colorado Plateau began to be pushed upwards as a result of the movement of the Earth's crust (see pages 32-35). As the crust moved, the rock was pushed upwards and squashed in a process called folding. The uplift of the plateau caused the Colorado River's speed to increase, which in turn caused it to cut through the rock more rapidly. The 2,334 kilometre long Colorado River begins its journey in the Rocky Mountains and travels all the way to the Gulf of California. During the ice ages (see pages 40-41), the wetter conditions meant that the river cut through the rock faster and deeper. Most of the down-cutting occurred between 5.3 and 1.2 million years ago.

### THE CANYON TODAY

The Colorado River still cuts across the canyon floor creating a narrow valley, eroding the cliff edges on its journey. But the river is not as great as it used to be. Even as recently as 100 years ago, it was much faster and more powerful than it is today. Decades of damming, diverting and drying up have taken their toll. Despite this, weathering, erosion and **transportation** are ongoing and we cannot be sure what the canyon may look like in the future.

### TEST YOURSELF

▶ Identify two layers from either of the photographs of the Grand Canyon and suggest how each layer could have formed.

# 4

# Resources from the Earth

Our planet, and the atmosphere that surrounds it, provide us with all we need to eat, drink, breathe, construct buildings, create computers and fuel our vehicles. While we often take the Earth's resources for granted, the whole of civilisation depends on them.

## MINERALS

Minerals are natural compounds formed through geological processes. There are currently over 4,000 known minerals on planet Earth. Rocks are aggregates of one or more minerals. Minerals can be pure elements, simple salts or very complex compounds with thousands of known forms. To be classed as a mineral, the substance must be a solid and have a crystalline structure. A crystalline structure is an orderly, repeating arrangement of atoms or molecules. Table salt is a mineral and has a crystal structure. In table salt, all of the sodium and chlorine particles are arranged in a repeating fashion. This pattern is termed 'cuboid'.

▼ Sodium chloride (salt) crystals form cubes.

## WHERE DO MINERALS COME FROM?

Many of the Earth's minerals originate from the molten mantle, beneath the Earth's crust. Natural processes, such as convection currents in the mantle, cause the material to come towards the surface of the Earth.

## MINING

When minerals are present in a rock in a quantity that makes extracting them financially worthwhile, the rock is called an ore. Our ancestors have been mining for thousands of years. The oldest mine is in Swaziland, in Africa, and is believed to be around 43,000 years old. Early humans mined for a mineral called haematite, which contains iron oxides and sometimes small amounts of titanium. They ground the haematite to obtain a pigment called red ochre, which was probably used for painting.

Today, geologists use both geological and chemical clues to locate mineral ores. They use sophisticated instruments to detect changes in magnetism, gravity and radioactivity. They analyse the chemical make-up of the ground and use their knowledge of the area's geology to locate minerals. If the geologists detect minerals, they mathematically calculate the quantity and quality of the mineral in the area. If it is worth extracting the mineral, retrieval of the ore will begin.

## RETRIEVING THE ORE

The two main types of mining are open pit mining and underground mining.

(1) Open pit mining is carried out if the mineral is within 200 metres of the Earth's surface, or if the rock is not hard and strong enough to support a tunnel. Heavy machinery digs and scrapes away the layers of soil and rock covering the ore. The walls of an open pit mine are graduated into benches, and the walls are not vertical. This helps to reduce rock falls. Gypsum, limestone and sandstone are excavated from open pit mines.

(2) Underground mining is carried out if the mineral is buried deep in the Earth's crust. Deep shafts called blast holes are drilled down into the crust. Benches are cut horizontally into the rock from the main shaft. Small quantities of explosives are placed along the benches. When the explosives are set off, the ore loosens and falls to the bottom of a long shaft. The ore is retrieved using either a

▼ The upper layers of this open pit copper mine in Utah, USA, have been stripped away to reveal the copper ore beneath.

## TIME TRAVEL: INTO THE FUTURE

▶ Humans do not only drill into the Earth to retrieve resources. An international team called the Integrated Ocean Drilling Program have been carrying out exploration work underneath the ocean, towards the centre of the Earth. So far, the team have successfully drilled through the majority of the crust beneath the ocean bed. They hope to gain clues about how new ocean crust material is formed. It has taken five months and 25 specialised drill bits made from hardened steel to penetrate 1.4 kilometres into the ocean floor. In the future, they want to extend the hole into the mantle for another 2.35 kilometres.

conveyor belt or skips which haul the rubble to the surface up a separate shaft. Collection of the rubble is either done manually, or controlled remotely to prevent injuries.

Underground mines provide hot, dirty and extremely dangerous work environments. Workers travel deep underground in caged lifts, and there is a constant risk of falling rocks and fire. In the USA, China, Russia, India, South Africa and Europe,

hundreds of coal mines are smouldering. Because of the size of the fires and because they are located deep beneath the Earth's surface, they are impossible to put out or to control.

### TREATING THE ROCKS

Once the rocks, such as limestone or metal ores, are removed from the mine, they are crushed and waste rock is discarded. Often, at least 30 per cent of the rock is discarded as waste material.

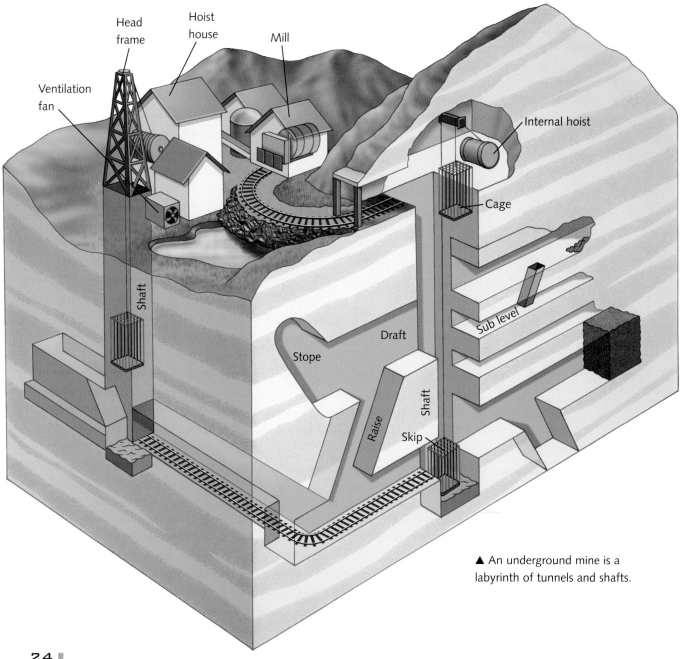

▲ An underground mine is a labyrinth of tunnels and shafts.

The remaining mixture is ground into a gravel-like consistency. Chemicals are added to the mixture to create a 'slurry', which is a lumpy liquid. The chemicals coat the desired minerals so that they float to the surface. The layer on the top of the slurry is skimmed off by a large mechanical arm.

## WHAT DO WE USE MINERALS FOR?

According to a survey in the USA, the average person consumes or uses 18,000 kilogrammes of minerals every year. In the course of a lifetime this could mean 476 kilogrammes of both lead and zinc, 488 kilogrammes of copper, 2,000 kilogrammes of aluminium and 453,000 kilogrammes of industrial products such as limestone. In fact, we are surrounded by minerals every day. Simple tasks like boiling a kettle to make a pot of coffee involve a number of minerals. The electric switch may be made from aluminium, copper and plastic, which is a product of oil. The coffee pot may be made from glass or ceramics both derived from minerals. The coffee beans themselves may even have been fertilised using minerals.

## DID YOU KNOW?

▶ Ammonium Nitrate Fuel Oil (ANFO) is the main explosive used in mineral mining. This explosive is capable of releasing 100,000 tonnes of rock in just one explosion – 100,000 tonnes of rock weighs roughly the same as 20,000 elephants!

▶ Some species of plant are capable of accumulating minerals in their tissues. When the Indian mustard plant is grown on soil rich in gold ore, it absorbs the gold into its tissues. If the crop is burned, and the ash analysed, a significant amount of gold can be retrieved. This alternative method of mining has other uses, too. Phyto-remediation is the use of plants to clear up contaminated areas of land. Sunflowers, oats, barley and dandelions take up heavy metal and chemical toxins from the soil, through their roots. They store the chemicals in their stems and leaves. These toxins do not seem to harm them. Eventually, the plants can be destroyed and the soil is left cleansed of the pollutants.

▶ **The Indian mustard plant is usually grown for use in cooking, but it can be used to take up gold from soil.**

The collection of gases that surrounds planet Earth is called the atmosphere. Most of the atmosphere (78 per cent) is made up of a chemically unreactive gas called nitrogen. Oxygen makes up around 21 per cent of the atmosphere. The remaining one per cent is a mixture of carbon dioxide, water vapour and argon. Since the formation of planet Earth, the atmosphere has evolved (changed gradually) over time.

### THE FIRST ATMOSPHERE

Planet Earth formed approximately 4.6 billion years ago from a vast cloud of dust and gas. Its original atmosphere was composed of hydrogen and helium. This is sometimes called the Earth's first atmosphere. By about 3.5 billion years ago, this atmosphere had been dispersed by the fierce heat of the Sun and by the heat radiating from the molten Earth.

▼ This image shows the Earth's atmosphere. The Earth is the lower dark area. The atmosphere includes the orange and blue regions and gradually disappears into space.

### THE SECOND ATMOSPHERE

As the molten Earth cooled down, its solid crust formed. However, the molten rock beneath frequently burst through the crust, and formed the earliest volcanoes. The volcanoes released gases into the atmosphere including ammonia, carbon dioxide, methane and steam. The Earth's second atmosphere formed. It was primarily carbon dioxide and steam, with a small amount of nitrogen. At this time, there was very little oxygen in the atmosphere. Humans could not have survived these conditions.

Over the next few billion years, the Earth cooled further still. The steam in the ancient atmosphere **condensed** to form rain and primitive oceans. Gradually, the oceans absorbed over 50 per cent of the atmosphere's carbon dioxide. The first life forms developed which are thought to have been bacteria-like. These were the first organisms to consume carbon dioxide and produce oxygen. Recently, scientists have isolated bacteria-like

organisms from deep sea vents at the bottom of the ocean. They are thought to be very similar to the earliest life forms found on Earth. Conditions around deep-sea vents, which are also called underwater volcanoes, are thought to represent those of the ancient, primitive oceans. They have high sulphur and salt concentrations, high temperatures and pressures, and a lack of oxygen.

▼ **This black smoker vent is over three kilometres below sea level.**

### THE THIRD ATMOSPHERE

Over the last 200 million years, the Earth's nitrogen- and oxygen-rich atmosphere developed. This formed the third atmosphere. Simple plant life evolved. Plants use carbon dioxide and water in a process called **photosynthesis**. Photosynthesis releases oxygen as a by-product, which meant that the oxygen content of the atmosphere gradually increased over millions of years, allowing more complex life forms to evolve. As oxygen was released, it reacted with ammonia to create nitrogen. Nitrogen was also released by primitive bacteria living in the soil. In the presence of ultraviolet light, such as that emitted by the Sun,

oxygen molecules combined to form ozone ($O_3$). The ozone layer in the atmosphere prevents harmful rays from the Sun reaching the Earth. The presence of the ozone layer meant that the surface was protected from harmful solar radiation, which permitted the evolution of animal life.

Today, the proportions of gases in our atmosphere are changing as a result of human actions. The levels of carbon dioxide are rising. Carbon dioxide acts like a blanket around the Earth and traps heat within the atmosphere. We call this the **greenhouse effect**. On the planet Venus, a natural runaway greenhouse effect has caused surface temperatures of over 400°C. All of Venus' surface water has evaporated, which has resulted in high levels of greenhouse gases in the atmosphere. The gases trapped massive amounts of heat and this caused Venus to become extremely hot.

▼ **Venus' atmosphere is 96.5 per cent carbon dioxide. It contains no oxygen.**

## USES OF ATMOSPHERIC GASES

Just like the Earth's crust, our atmosphere provides us with some important materials that are useful, and in some cases essential, for life.

(1) Nitrogen – The freezing point of nitrogen is almost -200°C. Liquid nitrogen is used to freeze many products, including food, and human tissues during the artificial fertilisation process. Nitrogen gas is also used in food storage. It is a very inert gas and will not react with food. Crisp packets are filled with nitrogen gas to prevent the food from coming into contact with oxygen and spoiling.

Nitrogen's unreactivity is also important in the movement of flammable and explosive substances. For example, when oil is pumped ashore from an oil rig, nitrogen gas is pumped alongside so that the oil is not exposed to oxygen, which could lead to an explosion.

▼ This huge explosion was caused by a liquid petroleum gas leak. It mixed with air, ignited and exploded.

(2) Oxygen – Oxygen is a much more reactive gas than nitrogen. It is essential to life and is breathed by animals, including humans.

(3) Carbon dioxide – Carbon dioxide is used for putting the fizz into fizzy drinks. It is a slightly soluble gas and forms bubbles in liquid. When fizzy drinks are left open to the atmosphere, they go 'flat' as the carbon dioxide escapes. Carbon dioxide can be cooled to form a solid called dry ice. It never forms a liquid at normal pressures, because carbon dioxide **sublimes**. This means it changes directly from a gas into a solid, without entering a liquid phase. Dry ice is used in stage smoke because when it heats up it produces an eerie smoke effect.

▶ This dry ice turned into gas when it was dropped in water.

Carbon dioxide is also used in fire extinguishers. When applied to a fire, it smothers the flame by depriving it of oxygen.

Under the correct conditions of temperature and pressure, carbon dioxide can form a liquid. Liquid carbon dioxide is used to make decaffeinated coffee. The coffee beans are soaked in baths of liquid carbon dioxide, which become saturated in caffeine. After decaffeination has occurred, the carbon dioxide is either drained off, or the pressure is reduced back down to normal levels and the carbon dioxide turns back into a gas.

# EARTH'S OCEANS

The oceans cover 71 per cent of the Earth's surface. Some scientists estimate that the oceans contain 50 million billion tonnes of dissolved solids. The oceans contain almost every known element. It is estimated that if all of the salts were removed from the oceans and spread on the land, they would form a layer as thick as a 40-storey building.

## WHY ARE THE OCEANS SALTY?

On average, seawater contains around 3.5 per cent salt. There are two main reasons why the oceans are salty:

(1) When the oceans first formed, sodium leached out of the ocean floor and chlorine gas entered the water through underwater volcanoes. This formed sodium chloride, which is the most abundant salt in the oceans.
(2) Rivers run across land, and as they do so, they pick up minerals. They deposit the minerals in the seas and oceans. Over millions of years, the **salinity** of the oceans increased. The Sun evaporates pure water from the oceans, and leaves the minerals behind.

Salinity is a measure of the saltiness of a body of water. Salinity varies from place to place, depending on the following factors:
▶ Ice cover
▶ Influx of river water
▶ Climatic factors such as wind, rain and evaporation
▶ Wave motion and ocean current

The ocean waters with the lowest salinity levels are found in areas where temperatures are cool, and where there is a large influx of river water.

The ocean waters with the highest salinity levels are found in hot parts of the world where evaporation rates are high and the influx of river water is low. In addition, polar seas have a high salinity because fresh water is frozen into icebergs, leaving behind the salt in the seawater.

The most salty water in the world is found in the Dead Sea, which is actually a salt water lake located in one of the lowest exposed points on the Earth's surface. The salinity is around 35 per cent. The Dead Sea is on the borders of Israel and Jordan. High temperatures and wind speeds mean that evaporation rates are high. When water evaporates, the minerals are left behind and the sea becomes more and more concentrated. Extensive irrigation and low rainfall in the region has also resulted in the high salt concentrations. Salty water is more buoyant than freshwater. The higher the salinity, the greater the buoyancy.

▼ The Dead Sea is very easy to float in because of its high salinity.

## RESOURCES FROM OCEAN WATER

Ocean waters are an important source of iodine and bromine. Iodine is a chemical element that is used as a disinfectant, a water sanitiser (cleaner) and as a medicine. Bromine is a very rare element. It has leached from the Earth's crust into seawater where it is present at concentrations of around 85 ppm (parts per million). The Dead Sea contains the world's highest natural concentrations of bromine at 5,000 ppm. Israel produces over 180,000 tonnes of bromine from the Dead Sea each year. It is vital to the pharmaceutical industry and is also used in fuel preparation, dyes, fire extinguishers and photographic film.

▼ Salt is evaporated from seawater on the island of Lanzarote in the Atlantic Ocean, 125 km off the coast of Africa.

## RESOURCES FROM THE OCEAN FLOOR

Scientists have attempted to mine materials from the ocean floor, including tin, gold, diamond, manganese and silver. But the mining techniques are currently too difficult and expensive to make sense commercially. The water pressure on the ocean floor is immense, and would crush a human.

Today, most of our minerals and resources are still extracted from land despite the abundance of the ocean's resources. For example, there are actually more diamonds under the ocean floor than there are under the continents. In the future, improved removal techniques may mean that ocean mining becomes a worthwhile pursuit.

## DID YOU KNOW?

▶ Scientists have discovered that certain species of marine plants and animals can be used to extract rare elements from seawater. For example, cobalt and radioactive plutonium have been found in the bodies of marine crayfish; copper has been found in oysters; and there is gold in the bodies of some jellyfish.

## FRESH WATER

Fresh water is found in rivers, streams and lakes, but it is not evenly distributed around the world. Around two billion people do not have enough fresh water. The United Nations declared a water crisis in 1990. Scientists are trying to find a way to distribute fresh water to all.

▼ This river's fresh water has come from a glacier in Kootenay National Park in Canada.

## DESALINATION

Desalination is a process that separates the salt from seawater. Obtaining fresh water from seawater has been carried out by seafarers since ancient times. However, industrial desalination plants were not built until the end of the 1800s. In the past, desalination was very expensive because it requires a great deal of electrical power.

Over the last 20 years, the plants have become more efficient and the price of desalinated water has decreased 100-fold. The most efficient installations can produce one cubic metre of fresh water for 10 cents (US). Today there are about 800 large desalination plants in the world, but this is not enough to provide everyone with the water they need, particularly in the developing world.

▶ This desalination plant is near the Caspian Sea.

## HOW DOES IT WORK?

There are two ways in which desalination can work.
(1) Distillation – The seawater is heated and evaporated. Water vapour rises, and leaves the salt behind. The water vapour is cooled. It condenses and is collected.
(2) Reverse osmosis – **Osmosis** is the movement of a substance, usually water, from an area where there is a lot of it, to an area where there is less, across a **semi-permeable membrane**. In reverse osmosis, the salt water is forced onto the membrane. The membrane only allows water to pass through it. Fresh water passes through and is collected. The salt is left behind.

# 5

# Our changing Earth

The Earth's crust is made up of pieces called tectonic plates. These plates float on the fluid mantle beneath and are positioned together like a badly-fitting jigsaw. The areas of land on which we walk are called **continental plates**. The areas of land underneath the oceans are called **oceanic plates**. A tectonic plate can be made partly of a continental plate and partly by an oceanic plate. The plates move gradually over time in a process called **plate tectonics**.

## CONTINENTAL DRIFT

This idea was first proposed in 1912 by a German scientist called Alfred Wegener. Wegener proposed that the continents were once joined, but over a period of millions of years they had drifted apart. We call this idea **continental drift**.

We now know that there are convection currents in the Earth's mantle and that these currents move in a circular motion. When solid objects float on fluids that contain convection currents, they move in a particular pattern.

### PLATE BEHAVIOUR

The Earth's crust is made of ten major tectonic plates and many minor ones. They meet at **plate boundaries**. Tectonic activity, such as earthquakes and volcanoes, occurs at the boundaries. On average, plates drift at between 2.5 and 15 centimetres per year. There are three ways in which plates move:

**(1) Plates that move towards each other** – The result of this kind of movement depends on the density of the plates involved. Oceanic plates are denser than continental plates, so when they meet, the denser oceanic plate slips underneath the continental plate. This is called **subduction**. Subduction is not usually smooth; instead it is sharp, sudden and violent. This can lead to earthquakes. Earthquakes are shock waves travelling through the Earth's crust. These can have disastrous results (see pages 36-37).

In some types of subduction, the oceanic plate sinks so low beneath the continental plate that the rock melts. Sometimes, this extra molten material leaves the mantle in the form of a volcano. When this happens, the oceanic plate is being broken down at the boundary between the two plates. This is called a **destructive boundary**.

## A DESTRUCTIVE BOUNDARY

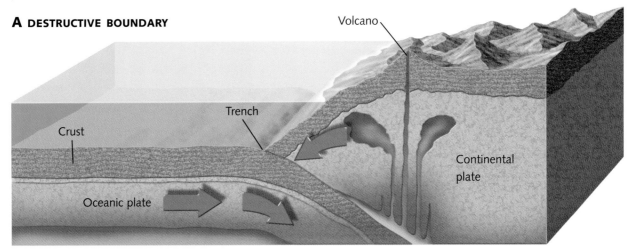

Volcano

Trench

Crust

Continental plate

Oceanic plate

When two plates of similar density move towards each other, the plates collide and push upwards. The rock crumbles and folds and produces mountain ranges. The Himalaya mountain range is an example of folded mountains.

### INVESTIGATE

Find a map in a library book or on the internet that shows the Earth's plates and the directions in which they move. Use this information to locate one of each of the following boundaries:

▶ Constructive
▶ Destructive
▶ Conservative

## MOUNTAIN FORMATION

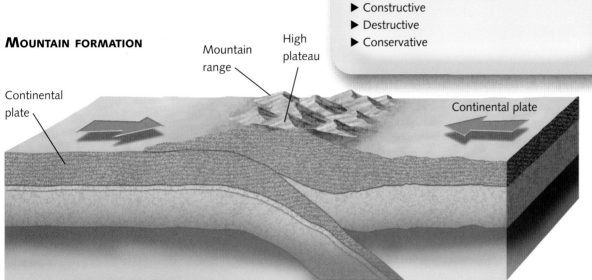

Continental plate

Mountain range

High plateau

Continental plate

**(2) Plates that move away from each other –** If plates move apart, molten magma comes to the surface to fill the gap. It cools and solidifies on the edges of the plates and makes new rock material. This is called a **constructive boundary**. If this process occurs between two oceanic plates, it is called sea floor spreading.

**(3) Plates that move alongside each other –** Some plates move in opposite directions, but parallel to each other. The edges of the plates are not usually smooth and the passing movements can be jerky and sudden. This movement can also cause earthquakes. Plates that move past each other in this way are called **conservative boundaries**.

## A CONSTRUCTIVE BOUNDARY

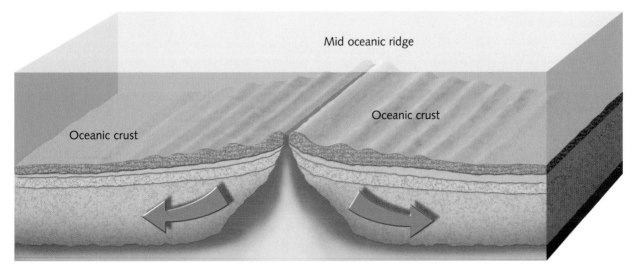

Mid oceanic ridge

Oceanic crust

Oceanic crust

The theory of plate tectonics is widely accepted by scientists. The Pakistan earthquake in 2005 and the south-east Asian tsunami in 2004 are both recent examples of how powerful the plates can be. We will now explore some of the evidence for plate tectonics.

## JIGSAW PIECES

When you look at the shapes of coastlines, it is easy to see that some edges look like the exact opposite of other edges, like two pieces of a jigsaw. In 1915, Alfred Wegener (see page 32) published this idea in his book, *The Origin of Continents and Oceans*. He described how the east coast of South America and the west coast of Africa looked as though they were once joined.

▲ Notice how the coasts of South America and Africa look as though they were once joined. Are there other coastlines that resemble each other in this way?

## ROCK STUDIES

This idea prompted geologists to study rocks on opposite sides of the oceans. They found rocks with identical, yet unusual, chemical structures and magnetic properties. They also studied fossils found in these locations. Elements decompose at a known rate. By measuring the decomposition of elements within the fossils, geologists pinpointed the rock's age to within a few hundred years. Fossils found in sedimentary rocks on opposite sides of the oceans are exactly the same in species and age. It is unlikely

that these ancient animals swam from one continent to another. The evidence suggests that in the past, the land masses must have been closer together, or else joined.

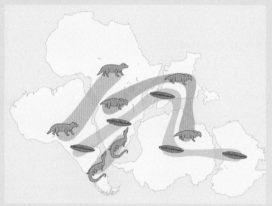

▲ When the continents were joined, animals could easily spread across what are now very distant landmasses.

## EVIDENCE FROM THE OCEAN FLOOR

In 1947, scientists discovered that the sediment layer on the floor of the Atlantic was much thinner than expected. Previously, scientists believed that the oceans were at least four billion years old. If this were true, the sediment layer would be much thicker. The evidence suggests that the ocean floor is a changing environment and relatively newly evolved.

In the 1950s, scientists found a great mountain range on the floor of the Atlantic Ocean. This global mid-ocean ridge is around 50,000 kilometres long and more than 800 kilometres wide. It zigzags between the continents, winding its way around the globe. Running along the top of this mountain range is a crack, called a rift valley. It is here that new ocean floor is forming. As the two mountain sides move away from each other, magma moves up between the plates and forms new ocean floor. This is termed ocean floor spreading and is an example of a constructive boundary.

In the years following World War II, continental oil reserves were being depleted rapidly and the search for offshore oil was on. In 1968, a group of scientists embarked on a year-long expedition, travelling back and forth across the Mid-Atlantic Ridge between South America and Africa, and drilling core samples at specific locations. What was found proved beyond doubt that sea floor spreading was occurring. Samples taken from set distances from the ridge were identical in composition and age.

## EARTHQUAKES

By the late 1920s, scientists were beginning to identify several prominent earthquake zones. They measured the shock waves produced by earthquakes on a seismograph. This machine enabled them to locate the epicentre of an earthquake. By plotting the epicentres on a map, it is clear that the majority of them are concentrated along specific lines. Scientists concluded that the earthquake zones correspond to the places where tectonic plates meet.

## ANCIENT CONTINENTS

By piecing together geological, chemical and physical data, scientists have concluded that the Earth's plates are constantly on the move. Over millions of years, the plates have separated and reformed several times:

| Supercontinent | Date of formation | Date of separation |
|---|---|---|
| Columbia | 1.8 billion years ago | 1.5 billion years ago |
| Rodinia | 1.3 billion years ago | 750 million years ago |
| Pannotia | 600 million years ago | 540 million years ago |
| Pangaea | 300 million years ago | 225 million years ago |

▼ When the epicentres of earthquakes are plotted on a map of the Earth, the plate boundary lines become clearly marked.

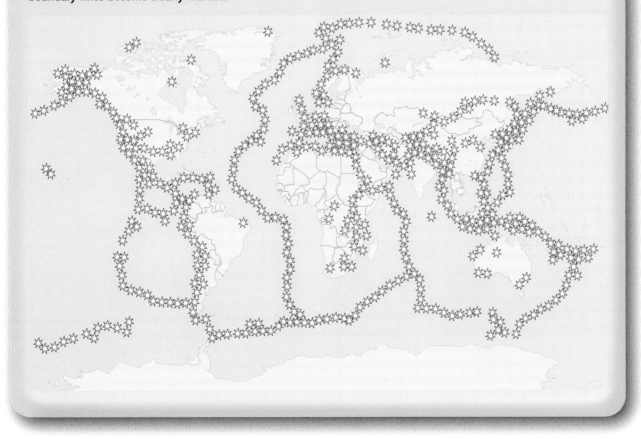

## PAKISTAN EARTHQUAKE

Earthquakes are estimated to occur on planet Earth every 11 seconds. Fortunately, most of these quakes are so small that we cannot feel them. But from time to time, massive earthquakes strike. In October 2005, a devastating earthquake hit northern Pakistan. The epicentre was 19 kilometres from the city of Muzaffarabad, and 26 kilometres beneath the surface. The earthquake caused widespread destruction and loss of life.

### THE RICHTER SCALE

Earthquakes are measured on the **Richter Scale**. The scale ranges from 1 to 10. The most powerful recorded earthquake occurred in Chile in 1960. It measured 9.5 on the Richter Scale.

### THE RICHTER SCALE

| NUMBER | EFFECTS | HOW OFTEN DO THEY OCCUR? |
|---|---|---|
| Less than 2 | None. These earthquakes are not felt. | 2,920,000 per year |
| 4 | Indoor items rattle. No significant damage. | 6,200 per year |
| 6 | Destructive. Causes damage to buildings in areas 160 km across. | 120 per year |
| 8 | Very destructive. Causes serious damage in areas several hundred km across. | 1 per year |
| 9 or above | Devastating in areas thousands of km across. | 1 every 20 years. |

### WHY DID THE EARTHQUAKE OCCUR?

The Pakistan earthquake measured 7.6 on the Richter scale. Northern Pakistan is on the boundary between the Eurasian and Indian plates. As the Eurasian and Indian plates tried to push towards each other, a massive amount of energy built up. Eventually the Earth's crust shifted suddenly and violently, and this caused the earthquake. The movement of these two plates over millions of years accounts for the presence of the Himalaya mountain range.

The energy from the earthquake was transferred through the Earth's crust as a shock wave. The shock waves of the earthquake were felt in several cities including the capital, Islamabad. There have been more than 1,500 after shocks since the earthquake.

▼ The Pakistan earthquake occurred on the boundary between the Eurasian and Indian plates. The red lines represent the plate boundaries.

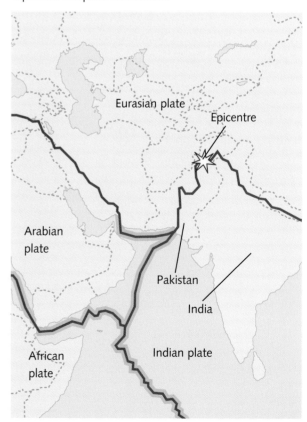

Eurasian plate

Epicentre

Arabian plate

Pakistan

India

African plate

Indian plate

▲ Part of this mountain collapsed when the earthquake struck.

## EFFECTS OF PAKISTAN'S EARTHQUAKE

As a result of the earthquake, whole towns and villages were wiped out, hundreds of thousands of buildings collapsed or sustained severe damage, and in the city of Muzaffarabad, close to the epicentre, over 50 per cent of all buildings were destroyed. This resulted in the deaths of over 90,000 people in Pakistan and India, and over 106,000 people were injured.

In addition, the United Nations estimate that around four million people were directly affected by the earthquake. Survivors struggled to cope because they were without homes or shelter, food or water. Heavy rain and consequent mudslides, the mountainous terrain and the onset of winter in the Himalayas made the rescue effort very tough. Mudslides carried away whole villages and buried some people who survived the initial earthquake, but remained trapped.

One of the other great threats following the earthquake was disease. A lack of fresh water and proper sanitation meant that diseases spread very quickly. Medication and medical expertise were also in short supply. Cholera, typhoid and tetanus were some of the most prominent threats. The international community donated more than 5.8 billion US dollars to help rescue survivors and rebuild the region, but there is still a long way to go.

## VOLCANOES

Volcanoes exist all over the world – usually along tectonic plate boundaries. Some volcanoes, such as those that formed the Hawaiian islands are nowhere near a plate boundary. These volcanoes are formed by 'hotspots'. A hotspot is an area that has experienced volcanic activity over a long period of time. There is much debate surrounding the cause of hotspots.

### HOTSPOTS

There are between 40 and 50 known hotspots on planet Earth. Hawaii, Réunion (an island in the Indian Ocean), Yellowstone National Park, the Galapagos Islands and Iceland lie over the most active hotspots. Some scientists believe that they are formed by stationary plumes of magma that well up from the mantle, and break through the Earth's surface. Other scientists have argued that their instruments show differences in the magma and mantle activity between hotspots. Instead, they think that hotspots are caused by plate tectonics, not plumes.

Interestingly, the chain of Hawaiian Islands formed as the Pacific plate moved over a hotspot.

The plate moves northwest at a rate of 52 kilometres every million years. The hotspot has remained stationary, and its eruptions have resulted in a line of islands. The islands in the far north-west are oldest and smallest because they have been eroded for longer. The newer and larger island are to the south-east.

### LAVA

When molten magma breaks through the crust, the material is called lava. Lava varies depending on the minerals and gases dissolved in it. For example, lava that contains silica is very viscous (thick) and will not spread a great distance. When silica is absent, the lava is less viscous and can flow freely over a much greater distance.

The viscosity of the lava inside a volcano determines the volcano's shape. If the lava is thin and runny, the volcano will be wide with shallow sides. These kinds of volcanoes release huge quantities of lava, which builds a wide mountain. The largest volcano of this type is Mauna Loa, which forms part of Hawaii. It is over 9,000 metres tall and is an incredible 120 kilometres in diameter.

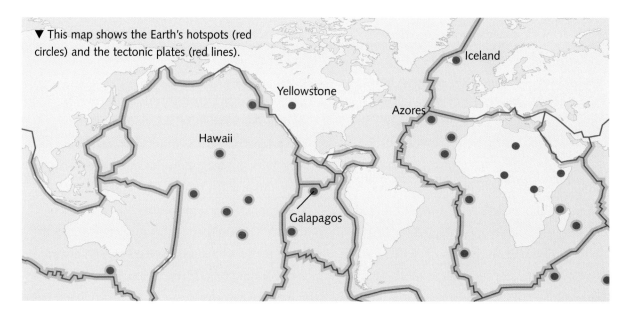

▼ This map shows the Earth's hotspots (red circles) and the tectonic plates (red lines).

Iceland

Yellowstone

Azores

Hawaii

Galapagos

If a volcano's lava is thick, it does not flow as freely or as far. It builds narrower volcanoes with steep sides. Steep-sided volcanoes are often extremely explosive. The pressure inside builds up and when released, a large amount of lava is forced through a narrow space.

▲ Mount Fuji in Japan generates thick lava.

## MOUNT PINATUBO

In 1991, Mount Pinatubo in the Philippines erupted with such tremendous force that over five cubic kilometres of material was expelled.

▼ Mount Pinatubo's eruption blasted away 150 metres of the volcano. It generated a massive cloud of ash.

The ash was ejected 34 kilometres up into the atmosphere. Ash particles rubbed together, which generated static electricity. This formed lightning bolts inside the ash cloud. The lava flowed 16 kilometres from the volcano, destroying buildings and killing over 300 people. It was one of the most powerful eruptions of the 1900s. However, compared to prehistoric eruptions, Mount Pinatubo was very weak.

## SUPERVOLCANOES

La Garita, a volcano in the San Juan Mountains in Colorado, USA, was the site of the largest ever volcanic eruption. The truly enormous eruption occurred 27 million years ago and was on an unimaginable scale. The caldera (collapsed remnant of the volcano) is 75 kilometres long and 35 kilometres wide and the explosion is thought to have released 5,000 cubic kilometres of material. The ash may have reached the east coast of North America and the Caribbean – over 3,000 kilometres. Luckily, this volcano is now extinct.

### DID YOU KNOW?

▶ Lava that contains little or no dissolved minerals can flow over an area of 100 square kilometres at a temperature of approximately 1,000°C.

# GLACIATION

A glaciation is also called an ice age. A glaciation is when ice sheets advance from each pole, towards the Equator. Glaciation is very different from a short-term change in our weather, such as a cold winter. Glaciation happens on a global scale over thousands or millions of years. There have been four major periods of glaciation in Earth's history, and many more minor glacial periods. The last minor glacial period ended 10,000 years ago, which is within human history. Over the last 700 years, the Earth's average temperature has fallen by 2°C which may indicate the approach of an ice age.

## WHY DOES THE EARTH COOL?

The most important factors are:

▶ **The Earth's orbit around the Sun** – This can change from a more circular orbit to a more oval one. If the orbit is very oval, the Earth will experience very cold winters, and cool summers. When the summers are so cool that ice from the previous winter does not retreat, this causes the onset of an ice age. The more ice that covers the Earth, the more the Sun's rays are reflected back into space off the Earth's white surface. This cools the Earth further still.

▶ **The energy emitted by the Sun (solar output)** – Solar output varies with time. When solar output is low, the Earth cools. Solar output increases and decreases over an 11 year cycle, but scientists also believe that the Sun has activity cycles that last hundreds or thousands of years.

▶ **Natural changes in the proportion of gases in our atmosphere** – Carbon dioxide acts as a blanket, and keeps warmth within the atmosphere. This causes warming – a natural greenhouse effect. However, the reverse of this, a decreased level of carbon dioxide, can cause cooling.

## HOW DOES THE ICE FORM?

As the Earth cools, winter snow remains for longer periods each year. Eventually, the snow cover lasts throughout the summer. Each year, the snow is compressed by further snowfall. Coupled with this, some of the surface snow can melt slightly and the melted ice seeps into the layers beneath. It fills in any air gaps and this creates a hard and dense ice.

## THE POWER OF ICE AGES

Glaciers can exert powerful forces on the materials around them. Ice can erode, transport and deposit sediments, which is similar to the effect that water has on land, but over a much longer period of time. During ice formation, layers build on top of each other. This exerts great pressure on the ice below. Eventually this pressure becomes so great, that the ice begins to move at the edges. The movement is enhanced by gravity; glaciers on steep mountain sides experience more movement than those on flatter land. The pressure also causes ice underneath the glacier to melt, which further oils the movement.

▼ The Franz Josef glacier on New Zealand's South Island is around 12 kilometres long. It flows from the Southern Alps into a temperate rainforest.

▲ The is the remaining Half Dome in Yosemite National Park, USA.

Material trapped in the ice, such as rock and gravel, rubs and erodes the surface over which the glacier travels. Some of the resulting scratches have been discovered and provide scientists with clues regarding glacier movement, including the direction of movement.

Glaciers also stick to rock faces. As the glacier moves, it can rip massive chunks of rock away. For example, a glacier carried away the missing half of the Half Dome in Yosemite National Park, USA.

Whole valleys can be shaped by glaciers through abrasion and erosion. Even today we can see this at work. The Rhone Valley in Switzerland is being constantly shaped by a slow moving tongue of ice.

## DID YOU KNOW?

▶ Some glaciers in Greenland can travel several kilometres a year.
▶ Scientists believe that the most severe glaciation, or ice age, occurred between 750 million and 580 million years ago. Ice covered the entire planet, creating a 'snowball Earth'. Even the oceans completely froze over.

# 6

# The driest places on Earth

Most deserts receive less than 25 centimetres of rainfall per year. This may occur all at once, or on separate occasions. Some deserts go for years with no rain at all. Deserts cover about 30 per cent of the Earth's surface. The Earth's largest desert is the Sahara Desert in North Africa. It covers 9,065,000 square kilometres, which is roughly the same size as the USA.

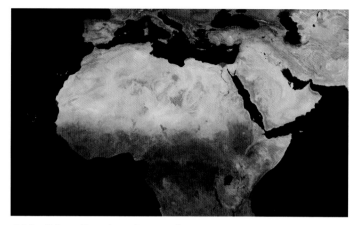

▲ The Sahara Desert can be seen from space.

## TYPES OF DESERT

Deserts are classified according to many factors, such as the number of days on which rain falls, temperature, humidity, location and wind. Some types of desert are described here:

### HOT AND DRY DESERTS

For most of the year these deserts are warm during the day, and sweltering in the summer months. There is little rainfall and humidity is very low. At night, the lack of water vapour in the atmosphere allows heat to escape and the temperature can plummet as low as -18°C.

Rainfall in this type of desert occurs in short bursts between long spells of drought. The problem is, because the ground is so hot, evaporation occurs at a faster rate than rain falls. Some rain even evaporates before it hits the ground. An example of this type of desert is the Sahara Desert in Africa, which receives only 1.5 centimetres of rain per year.

### TRADE WIND DESERTS

The trade winds blow towards the Equator from the Northern and Southern Hemispheres. They are hot and drying and they remove the cloud cover over regions 30° above and below the Equator. This allows more of the Sun's energy to reach and heat up the land. The Sahara Desert is formed by the trade winds.

▼ The trade winds blow towards the Equator and create very dry regions.

Trade winds

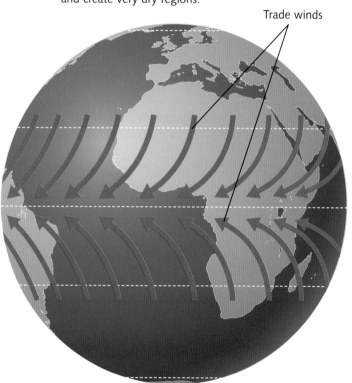

## SEMI-ARID DESERTS

Semi-arid deserts receive between 25 and 50 centimetres of rain each year and are found in North America, Europe and northern Asia. The summers are long and dry and the winters have very little rain; in fact precipitation is mostly in the form of snow in high areas. The temperature variation is usually between 10°C and 27°C. Dew forms during the night, supplementing the rainfall.

## COASTAL DESERTS

These deserts are found on the western edges of continents, such as Chile, western Australia, and south-western Africa. Coastal deserts are not hot. They have cool winters, warm summers and little rainfall. Their formation is caused by a complex interaction between oceanic, atmospheric and terrestrial (land related) systems.

## RAIN SHADOW DESERTS

These deserts form when tall mountains prevent moisture-rich clouds from reaching the far side of the mountains. As moist air rises over the mountains, the water vapour condenses into clouds. Eventually it falls on the tops of the mountains either as rain or snow, leaving the far side dry. The Himalayas play an important part in the formation of deserts in central Asia, such as the Taklamakan and Gobi deserts.

## MONSOON DESERTS

If there is a large temperature difference between a continent and the surrounding ocean, a monsoon wind will result. Monsoon winds are strong. The monsoon patterns around India are responsible for dumping a deluge of rain in short periods of time on the land. As large amounts of rain are dumped in one place, another region often suffers from a lack of rain which causes deserts to form. The Rajasthan Desert of India, and the Thar Desert of Pakistan are monsoon deserts.

## COLD DESERTS

These deserts have an annual rainfall between 15 and 26 centimetres and their summer temperature rarely gets above 10°C. They have short summers followed by long, cold winters. Cold deserts, also called polar deserts, cover over five million square kilometres of planet Earth. They are found in the Arctic, which includes parts of the USA, Canada, Russia, Norway, Sweden, Finland and Iceland, and the Antarctic. They can either be covered by ice and snow, or they can be tundra. Tundra landscapes are treeless plains that remain frozen solid for much of the year.

▼ This coastal tundra is on the island of Fugloya, 800 km north of Norway.

## HOW DO DESERTS FORM?

Desertification is when once-fertile land turns into desert. Deserts expand and shrink as a result of natural processes over thousands of years, but man's action can speed up desert formation:

(1) When land is overgrazed, or overused, plant life is lost.

(2) Plants hold soil together, and once they are gone, the land is more susceptible to erosion by wind and rain.

(3) The top layer of soil disappears.

(4) There is usually a lack of shade in areas undergoing desertification. This increases the evaporation rate of water, which draws salt up to the surface.

(5) Salt prevents further plant life from growing.

Desertification is particularly widespread in China. China's rural human population and livestock population have increased enormously over the last 60 years. The Gobi Desert is expanding at a rate of 2,460 square kilometres a year and massive dust storms are becoming more frequent. To counteract this desertification, the government want to plant a 'Green Wall' of forest trees in north-eastern China. The wall will be 5,700 kilometres long – much longer than the famous Great Wall of China. Chinese officials say that by 2050, much of the arid land will be restored.

Others are less hopeful. They say that it will not work because many of the trees will die and those that survive will soak up large amounts of water, which could increase desertification.

▼ Around one million tonnes of Gobi Desert sand blows into Beijing, China, each year.

### TEST YOURSELF

What types are the following deserts? Use the clues to help you to decide.

▶ Death Valley. This desert is surrounded by the Black Mountains.
▶ Antarctica. Here, the temperature is very low all year around.
▶ Deserts of Utah, Montana and Nevada. Summers here are long but winters can bring rain.

# TIME TRAVEL: DEATH VALLEY

Death Valley National Park is a rain shadow desert and receives less than 50 centimetres of rain a year. It is certainly the hottest, driest and lowest place in the USA. The highest recorded temperature was a staggering 56.7°C and the lowest recorded temperature was –9.4°C.

## FORMATION OF THE VALLEY

The oldest rock in Death Valley is 1.7 million years old and formed at a time when life on Earth was restricted to single-celled organisms, such as bacteria. Between 1.2 billion and 800 million years ago, marine deposition occurred. Western USA was a warm and tropical sea. When the clams, snails and sea stars that lived in the sea died, they fell to the sea floor and mixed with sand and silt. After 350 million years, six kilometres of sediment had been deposited. Many of the exposed rocks in Death Valley were formed by these marine creatures, and it is not unusual to find fossils from this era.

## VOLCANOES AND MOUNTAINS

The next stage in the formation of Death Valley was one of the most dramatic. Between 250 million and 65 million years ago, subduction occurred on the western side of the valley. High temperatures and immense pressures melted the rock. Some of the magma cooled beneath the surface and formed the intrusive igneous rock, granite. Some magma erupted through the Earth's surface and formed lava flows, which can still be seen today. The lava formed extrusive igneous rock which contained precious minerals, such as gold and silver.

▼ Ancient lava flow in Death Valley, USA.

## EROSION AND SPREADING

The volcanoes and mountains from this era were eroded over millions of years. Around 16 million years ago, the crust under North America began to spread and stretch apart. Between two and three million years ago, the stretching reached the Death Valley area and formed the Death Valley basin. It filled with sediment washed down from the surrounding mountains, and during the ice ages, it filled with water. Around 10,500 years ago, the valley became cut off from the melted water from the glaciers in the Sierra Nevada mountains and the desert formed.

## DEATH VALLEY TODAY

At 86 metres below sea level, the Badwater Basin in Death Valley is the lowest point in the Western Hemisphere. It contains minerals washed down from the surrounding mountains and salt from the evaporation of ancient lakes. The Earth's crust in this area is still spreading, and no-one knows for certain how this area will look thousands of years from now.

▼ The salt-encrusted Death Valley basin.

# Glossary

**CONDENSE** – To change from a gas to a liquid.

**CONSERVATIVE BOUNDARY** – A boundary between plates where crust is neither formed nor destroyed.

**CONSTRUCTIVE BOUNDARY** – Boundary between plates where new crust material is formed.

**CONTINENTAL DRIFT** – Movement of oceanic or continental plates on the Earth's surface.

**CONTINENTAL PLATE** – A plate that forms the Earth's continents. One plate may be partly continental and partly oceanic.

**CONVECTION CURRENT** – Movement created by hot material rising, cooling and then falling again.

**DESTRUCTIVE BOUNDARY** – Boundary between plates where crust material is destroyed.

**EROSION** – The wearing away of land through natural processes, such as water, wind, ice, or gravity.

**GEOLOGIST** – A person who studies the science of the Earth.

**GREENHOUSE EFFECT** – The warming of a planet, such as the Earth, caused by a blanket of greenhouse gases that prevent heat from escaping into space.

**IGNEOUS ROCK** – Rock formed from cooling molten magma.

**KELVIN** – A unit of temperature. 0K is absolute zero and is equal to -273.15°C.

**LAVA** – Molten magma that is expelled from a volcano.

**MAGMA** – Molten rock beneath the Earth's surface.

**METAMORPHIC ROCK** – Rock formed under intense heat and pressure.

**NUCLEAR FUSION** – Joining together of nuclei.

**OCEANIC PLATE** – A plate that forms the Earth's surface underneath the oceans.

**OSMOSIS** – Movement of a solvent from an area where there is a lot of it to an area where there is little, through a semi-permeable membrane.

## ANSWERS

**p9 Test yourself**

Layers of sediment are formed in three ways.
1. When the weathered remains of other rocks are deposited.

2. When the remains of plants and animals. are deposited.

3. When the liquid part of a solution, such as seawater, evaporates to leave behind a layer of sediment.

The layers build on top of one another and become compressed to form sedimentary rock. Sedimentary rocks include coal (a biogenic sedimentary rock), halite (a precipitate sedimentary rock) and sandstone (neither biogenic or precipitate).

**p13 Test yourself**

Igneous rocks form when magma (molten rock) from beneath the Earth's surface cools and solidifies. The rock can cool underground or above the ground.

When rock cools underground it is called intrusive igneous rock. It cools because it moves towards the cooler surface of the Earth, but without breaking through the surface.

When rock cools above the ground it is called extrusive igneous rock. It cools because it has been expelled from under the ground, often through a volcano, where it meets cooler air or water.

**p19 Investigate**

Porous rock contains tiny holes, or pores. Non-porous rock does not contain pores. Non-porous rock is better for building because it is less susceptible to attack by wind, rain and chemicals.

**p21 Test yourself**

Red layers can clearly be seen in the photograph. These sections contain a lot of iron that has leached from surrounding rocks.

White layers can also be observed. These are rich in limestone (calcium carbonate) formed from dead sea animals.

**PHOTOSYNTHESIS** – The process during which green plants use sunlight to convert carbon dioxide and water into energy and oxygen.

**PLASMA** – An extremely hot gas that is composed of atomic nuclei stripped of electrons and free electrons.

**PLATE BOUNDARY** – Where two tectonic plates meet.

**PLATE TECTONICS** – The theory that the Earth's crust is made of plates that float around on the Earth's molten interior.

**RECRYSTALLISATION** – When atoms or molecules of a rock or mineral are packed closer together to create a new crystal structure. This usually occurs under conditions of intense temperature and pressure.

**RICHTER SCALE** – A measure of earthquake strength on a scale from 0 to 10. This is a logarithmic scale. This means that a magnitude 7 earthquake is ten times more powerful than a magnitude 6 earthquake.

**SALINITY** – A measure of the amount of salt dissolved in water.

**SEDIMENTARY ROCK** – Rock made from millions of tiny sediments.

**SEMI-PERMEABLE MEMBRANE** – A membrane that allows only certain substances to pass through it.

**SUBDUCTION** – When one tectonic plate passes underneath another tectonic plate.

**SUBLIME** – To turn directly from a solid into a gas or vice versa.

**SUPERNOVA** – The explosion of a massive star at the end of its life.

**TRANSPORTATION** – The movement of small sediment material to alternative locations through natural processes.

**WEATHERING** – The breakdown of rock through physical and chemical processes.

## Useful websites:
http://www.chem4kids.com
http://www.howstuffworks.com
http://news.bbc.co.uk/1/hi/sci/tech
http://en.wikipedia.org/wiki/Main_Page
http://www.newscientist.com

**p31 Investigate**
The water on the plate should not taste salty.

The salt water has boiled and steam has formed. Steam is the evaporation product of the salt water. Steam contains only water molecules and no salt molecules. The salt has been left behind in the pan.

If the pan is left in a warm place, eventually all of the water will evaporate and only salt crystals will remain.

**p33 Investigate**
Example answers:
Constructive boundary – The Great Rift Valley has formed as a result of the separation of the African and Arabian tectonic plates. It is 5,000 kilometres long and runs from northern Syria in south-west Asia to central Mozambique in East Africa. The Arabian plate and two parts of the African plate (the Nubian and the Somalian) are moving away from each other.

Destructive boundary – The Andes Mountains have formed as a result of the collision between the Nazca Plate and the South American Plate.

Conservative boundary – The boundary between the Pacific Plate and the North American Plate is conservative. The Pacific Plate is pushing north and the North American Plate is pushing south. It has created the San Andreas fault, which runs 1287 kilometres through western and southern California in the United States.

**p44 Test yourself**
Death Valley is a rain shadow desert. We know this because it is surrounded by the Black Mountains.

Antarctica is a cold or polar desert. We know this because the temperatures are very low here.

The deserts of Utah, Montana and Nevada are semi-arid. We know this because the summers are long and hot but winters can bring rain. They receive slightly more rain than hot deserts.

# Index

Page references in italics represent pictures.